C0059 20993

 Glasgow libraries

Bridgeton Library
The Olympia Building
2-16 Orr Street
Glasgow G40 2QH
Phone/Fax: 0141 276 0870

This book is due for return on or before the last date shown below. It may be renewed by telephone, personal application, fax or post, quoting this date, author, title and the book number

1 1 MAY 2015

WITHDRAWN

1 8 APR 2017

D1059879

Glasgow Life and it's service brands, including Glasgow Libraries, (found at www.glasgowlife.org.uk) are operating names for Culture and Sport Glasgow

ER

AMBERLEY

Acknowledgements

Although most of the photographs that I have assembled here are my own, a big thank you must go to Graeme Blair, David Crichton, Jules Hathaway, Ian Leven, Walter Burt and the custodians of the railway photographs of the late David Murray for providing images from their collections. I also included one of my late father's photos. An extra thank you must go to my good friend of almost fifty years, Graeme Blair, for his help and encouragement, and in particular for obtaining photographs that I was unable to take due to work commitments.

The Railways of Fife by William Scott Bruce and the Rail Scot and Six Bells Junction websites have also been invaluable for obtaining information. Final thanks to my daughter Katie for proofreading my manuscript.

Front cover top: K4 2-6-0 No. 61994 *The Great Marquess* hurries through Ladybank, with its support coach, en route to Thornton in April 2010.

Front cover bottom: First Scot Rail Class 170 170421 departs Dunfermline Town station with a Fife Circle service to Glenrothes with Thornton in August 2014.

Back cover top: This bridge spans the trackbed of the Fife & Kinross Railway between Auchtermuchty and Strathmiglo. Fifty years after the line's closure the bridge is still owned by the British Railways Board.

Back cover bottom: The overgrown track of the Braeside Junction–Crombie branch.

Glasgow Life Glasgow Libraries	
B	
C 006140378	
Askews & Holts	25-Feb-2015
385.094129 S	£14.99

WITHDRAWN

First published 2015

Amberley Publishing
The Hill, Stroud, Gloucestershire, GL5 4EP
www.amberley-books.com

Copyright © Michael Mather, 2015

The right of Michael Mather to be identified as the Author of this work has been asserted in accordance with the Copyrights, Designs and Patents Act 1988.

ISBN 978 1 4456 4537 7 (print)
ISBN 978 1 4456 4539 1 (ebook)

All rights reserved. No part of this book may be reprinted or reproduced or utilised in any form or by any electronic, mechanical or other means, now known or hereafter invented, including photocopying and recording, or in any information storage or retrieval system, without the permission in writing from the Publishers.

British Library Cataloguing in Publication Data.
A catalogue record for this book is available from the British Library.

Typesetting by Amberley Publishing.
Printed in Great Britain.

A Brief History and Introduction

By the end of the nineteenth century, Fife, like most of central Scotland, had a fairly extensive railway network serving the towns and countryside, moving the people and products of its varied industries and agriculture around. But one must go back more than 100 years earlier to the beginnings of the railways in Fife.

These first railways were the Fordell and Charlestown wagonways to the south-east and south-west of Dunfermline, both using horse-drawn wagons to transport coal and limestone. The Fordell system transported coal from the pits on the Fordell estate down to St David's Harbour near Inverkeithing.

The Charlestown line, which eventually extended up to the south of Dunfermline, carried coal and limestone from pits and quarries on the Earl of Elgin's estate to the limekilns and harbour at Charlestown. In 1838, the Charlestown line became the first in Fife to carry fare-paying passengers, and this continued until 1863 when the line closed for rebuilding into a conventional railway. The line, although disused, is still in existence today, apart from the last half-mile to Charlestown harbour.

The Fordell line also became a conventional railway with its own fleet of steam locomotives, and was connected to the North British Railway at Crossgates. It closed in 1946.

It was in 1847 that the main line as we know it opened. Operated by the Edinburgh & Northern Railway it initially ran from Burntisland to Cupar and Lindores, eventually extending to Tayport and Perth. Passengers travelling from Edinburgh would first board a ferry at Granton, which would take them across the Forth to Burntisland where they would then board the train. Upon arrival at Tayport they would board another ferry to take them across the Tay to Dundee.

It wasn't until 1878 that the Tay was bridged, but this was to be short-lived following the collapse of its centre section at the end of the following year. The replacement bridge was opened in 1887. With the opening of the first Tay Bridge a new line was also opened from Leuchars Junction to Wormit at the south end of the bridge, and the line to Tayport was extended to Wormit.

Two years after the opening of the main line, a branch from Thornton Junction to Dunfermline was opened, terminating at what was to become Dunfermline Upper, now the site of B&Q. The present Dunfermline Town station, or Lower as it was called, opened in 1877 on a line that ran from North Queensferry Pier. This line was connected to the Thornton line at Townhill Junction, the present site of Dunfermline Queen Margaret station. The section from North Queensferry to Inverkeithing was superseded when the Forth Bridge opened.

With the opening of the Forth Bridge and the connecting line to Burntisland in 1890, the main line was complete, and it was now possible to travel all the way from London to Aberdeen by train.

The last line I shall mention here is the one from Kincardine to Dunfermline, which opened as late as 1906, linking up with the reopened Charlestown branch at Elbowend junction.

Almost all of the lines in Fife except colliery and industrial lines eventually came under the control of the North British Railway, later the LNER, then British Railways and now Network Rail.

Space does not permit covering the many other lines in Fife, so I have concentrated on the ones that are still open.

For over 100 years steam locomotives were the principle form of motive power, and many different types, both large and small, worked in Fife. The unsung heroes were the small goods and shunting engines that worked away day in and day out moving the county's goods around. Of course, there were the glamour locomotives too, the North British Atlantics, LNER Pacifics and the P2 2-8-2s.

While it is still possible to see an LNER Pacific in Fife, you won't see an Atlantic or P2, as they have all been scrapped, but this is about to change, as work has started on building a new P2. These powerful and impressive locomotives were built specifically to work the heavy trains between Edinburgh and Aberdeen, and all had appropriate Scottish names, *Cock of The North* and *Thane of Fife* to name two. Hopefully in a few years' time it will be possible to see this locomotive powering through Fife.

Freight, in particular coal from the many pits in Fife, was the principle form of revenue for the railway, and while many lines and stations lost their passenger services as early as the 1920s, freight continued for many years after.

Locomotive-hauled passenger trains were the norm until 1960 when the first diesel multiple units arrived. These soon took over the local services from the steam locomotives, while the arrival of Class 26 and Class 40 diesels meant the writing was on the wall for steam, as they took over both freight and the Edinburgh–Aberdeen passenger trains.

As more new classes of diesel locomotives arrived, steam was taking a back seat and had disappeared by 1967.

The Beeching report had its effect on Fife, too, and although there had been line and station closures prior to this, more were to follow. By the time steam had finished, many of the lines that it ran on had closed too.

This is where my book starts, covering the end of steam to the present day. My age is against me for anything much earlier, resulting in me having few good photographs of steam in Fife; I preferred to keep my precious pocket money-bought film for more exotic locations such as 'Perth', where it would be possible to photograph an A4 or Britannia Pacific.

I have tried to give a good cross section of the railway over the last forty-seven years – what has come and gone over the period from a nationalised to a privatised railway. It is a warts-and-all portrayal weather wise, though; as nice as Fife is, the sun doesn't always shine!

So let me take you on a rail trip through Fife, calling at all stations, first on the main line, then the Dunfermline branch and finally the Perth line, before looking at freight, closed lines, preservation and steam specials.

Michael Mather
October 2014

For anyone travelling to Fife by rail, the entry into the county couldn't be more spectacular than crossing the Forth Bridge, particularly when in the cab of A4 Pacific No. 60009 *Union of South Africa*. The locomotive is making its way across the bridge to Dunfermline, hauling an SRPS special in April 1985.

Ex-NBR J36 No. 65288 stands at Dunfermline shed in June 1966. This 1890s veteran and its Thornton-based classmate No. 65345 were destined to be the last two operating steam locomotives in Scotland when withdrawn in May the following year, outlasting all the more modern steam locomotives. (Walter Burt)

It is April 1967, one month before the end of steam in Scotland, at Dunfermline sheds, but for WD 2-8-0 No. 90386 the end has come, and it has only one more journey to make – to the scrapyard. These powerful, rugged locomotives had done sterling work in Fife over the years.

In May 1967, one year after being withdrawn from service, A4 Pacific No. 4498 *Sir Nigel Gresley* made a return visit to Scotland. Now preserved and painted in its original LNER garter blue livery, it worked a special from Glasgow to Aberdeen and return. It is seen here at Lochmuir Summit.

Traction Inspector Jock Buchanan surveys the scene from the cab of A3 Pacific No. 4472 *Flying Scotsman* at Inverkeithing station in May 1968. The locomotive was working a special from Stockton to Dunfermline and return. This was the last steam working in Fife before the end of BR steam in August 1968. (Matthew Mather)

7

On a misty day on the Forth in May 1973, two Class 101 Metropolitan Cammell DMUs pass on the Forth Bridge. These units performed the bulk of the local services in Fife from the 1960s to the 1980s.

Class 150 No. 150252 enters North Queensferry station on its way to Edinburgh in June 1999. The 150s were the first of the second generation of DMUs to work in Fife, arriving in the late 1980s. North Queensferry Tunnel started life as a cutting, but, because of rockfalls, it was roofed over.

Looking very smart in its early BR blue livery, A1 Pacific No. 60163 *Tornado* crosses Jamestown Viaduct on the climb to the Forth Bridge, hauling an SRPS Forth Circle rail tour in June 2013. Completed in 2008, the locomotive was built to the same design as the original LNER A1 Pacifics, all of which were scrapped in the 1960s.

Inverkeithing station is both a mix of old and new, with a modern main building and the original North British waiting room on the Up platform. An East Coast HST departing for Aberdeen completes the scene in August 2014.

In summer, many of Fife's stations have beautiful floral displays, often sponsored by local organisations. With a colourful foreground, First Scot Rail Class 158 No. 158731 waits to depart from Inverkeithing with a Fife Circle service to Glenrothes with Thornton in August 2014.

A Class 101 Metropolitan Cammell DMU passes under the B981 road bridge at Inverkeithing East Junction with a service to Edinburgh Waverley in May 1973. The line branching off to the left links up with the Inverkeithing–Dunfermline line, forming the top of the Inverkeithing Triangle.

LMS Duchess Pacific No. 46233 *Duchess of Sutherland* passes through Dalgety Bay station with an SRPS Forth Circle rail tour in September 2014. The station is one of Fife's newest, opening in 1998, and is near the former Donibristle halt. The Fordell Railway passed under the main line near this point.

Aberdour is a delightful station which has won many awards for its floral displays, and is seen at its best here in July 2014. Note the stone-built signal box beyond the footbridge, still standing thirty-four years after closure. This is the only closed signal box on the main line through Fife that is still standing.

A two-car Gloucester Railway Carriage and Wagon DMU departs Aberdour for Kirkcaldy in May 1973, a change from the more usual Class 101.

Above: This is the original terminus of the Edinburgh & Northern Railway at Burntisland, seen in June 2014. From here trains would depart for the north. The replacement station that can just be seen to the right was opened in 1890 when the new line from the Forth Bridge was completed. The terminus is still in use as office accommodation.

Right: This plaque, photographed in June 2014, commemorates the ferries that crossed the Forth. The train ferry carried goods wagons and was known as the floating railway. It was designed by Thomas Bouch, who would later go on to design the ill-fated first Tay Bridge.

BURNTISLAND'S FIRST STATION WAS OPENED IN 1847 BY THE EDINBURGH AND NORTHERN RAILWAY, WITH A FERRY TO GRANTON AND THENCE BY TRAIN TO EDINBURGH. THE WORLD'S FIRST TRAIN FERRY SERVICE STARTED ON THIS ROUTE IN 1850. IT ENDED IN 1890 WHEN THE FORTH BRIDGE OPENED WITH A NEW LINK LINE TO BURNTISLAND ON WHICH THE PRESENT STATION WAS BUILT.

THIS PLAQUE WAS ERECTED TO MARK THE REFURBISHMENT OF BURNTISLAND STATION JANUARY 1986

A4 Pacific No. 60009 *Union of South Africa* powers through Burntisland on a dull Sunday morning with an SRPS Forth Circle rail tour in April 2014. These steam-hauled tours, which take in the Fife Circle and Dunfermline–Alloa line, run a couple of Sundays a year, with two trips each day.

Kinghorn station, like many of the stations in Fife, is unstaffed most of the time. All of the stations have surplus space, some of which is rented out, and in Kinghorn's case part of the station, seen here in June 2014, is now a studio and gallery.

The Fife Coastal Path stretches for 117 miles from Kincardine to Newburgh, and is adjacent to the railway between North Queensferry and Kirkcaldy. As can be seen in this June 2014 photograph, the view across the Forth to Inchkeith Island and the Lothians is beautiful.

A First Scot Rail Class 170 No. 170429 departs Kinghorn with a Dundee–Edinburgh service in June 2014. This set is in the new Scot Rail livery, which will remain the same whichever company holds the franchise.

With two of Kirkcaldy's many linoleum factories behind, a Metropolitan Cammell Class 101 DMU stands at the town's station with a service to Leven in September 1967. All bar one of the town's factories have gone, as has the passenger service to Leven, which ceased in 1969.

A pair of BRCW Class 26s arrive at Kirkcaldy with an Inverness–Edinburgh service in August 1976. This train would have travelled over the Ladybank–Perth line, a practice that had started the year before. Kirkcaldy station was rebuilt in the 1960s, and the main building was rebuilt again in the late 1980s, following a fire.

Partially hidden by bushes, a First Scot Rail four-car Class 158 passes by Kirkcaldy's, and Britain's, last remaining linoleum factory, owned by Forbo Nairn.

Sinclairtown signal box sat above Factory Road in Kirkcaldy and controlled Sinclairtown goods yard. This shot was taken in 1975, five years before the box closed. No doubt the 1970 Foden is long gone too.

Sinclairtown station closed in 1969, but, as can be seen in this photograph, taken in September 2014, the façade still stands; its only purpose now is acting as a wall above the railway.

In September 2014, a First Scot Rail Class 170 speeds past the site of Sinclairtown station, which was below the level of St Clair Street. The two steel beams once supported the station building.

Thornton station signal box was one of the largest in Fife. It controlled the north junction, station and the line to Leven. In its heyday two signalmen per shift were required to work the box. This 1975 shot was taken six years after the closure of Thornton station. The box closed in 1980.

With Markinch and the East Lomond Hill in the background, a GNER HST approaches Coaltown of Balgonie while working an Aberdeen–London King's Cross service in March 2001. GNER were the first company to hold the East Coast franchise after privatisation, but lost it to National Express in 2007 after encountering financial difficulties.

Left: Andrew Barclay Class 06 Shunter No. D2438 rests between duties in front of Markinch goods shed in September 1969. The shunter was employed shunting the yard and trip workings down the Auchmuty branch to the Tullis Russell paper mill. In 1974 the goods shed became home to A4 Pacific No. 60009 *Union of South Africa.*

Below: The same view in 2014; the shed has gone, burnt down in a suspicious fire. In its place are a new ticket office, a wheelchair-accessible footbridge and a bus interchange. Space has also been left for a line into the bay platform.

A GNER HST races across Markinch Viaduct with a London King's Cross–Aberdeen service on a sunny evening in June 2006.

West Coast Railways Class 37s No. 37685 *Loch Arkaig* and No. 37516 *Loch Laidon* climb the 1 in 102 gradient from Markinch to Lochmuir Summit with 'The Royal Scotsman' luxury train in April 2014. On the first day of the classic four-day tour, it is travelling to Keith, where it will spend the night.

A misty day at Lochmuir Summit in June 1979 sees English Electric Class 37 No. 37052 passing with an Edinburgh–Inverness train, unusual motive power for one of these trains, particularly given that this locomotive was based at March in Cambridgeshire. (Graeme Blair)

The same scene in June 2003; the loop, signals and box have gone, having been closed in 1980. In this view of a Virgin Cross Country HST you would hardly know that the loop ever existed, such has been the growth of vegetation in the intervening years.

With about a mile to go, this Class 101 Metropolitan Cammell DMU has just passed through Falkland Road station on the southbound climb to Lochmuir Summit with a Dundee–Edinburgh service in June 1973.

Falkland Road station closed to passengers in 1958 and freight in 1964. This InterCity HST makes a fine sight as it passes through on its way to London King's Cross in April 1980, a sight still to be seen thirty-four years on. The station was demolished in the late 1990s.

Edinburgh Haymarket-based English Electric Class 40 No. D359 climbs the 1 in 95 Falkland Road Bank with an Aberdeen–Edinburgh Waverley express on a sunny June evening in 1973. Together with Haymarket's allocation of Brush Class 47s, they shared the work on the Aberdeen trains at this time.

It is 5.30 on a June 2014 morning and the sun is just above the horizon as DBS Class 67 No. 67011 coasts down Falkland Road Bank with the Aberdeen portion of the 'Caledonian Sleeper' from London Euston. The train splits at Edinburgh, with other portions going to Fort William and Inverness.

With the appropriately named Station Hotel beyond the bridge, a First Scot Rail Class 158 crosses Station Road in July 2012, and is about to pass the site of Kingskettle station, which closed in 1967. Note the bricked-up entrance on the left, from where steps led up to the platform.

This Class 221 Arriva Cross Country set has just departed Ladybank and is crossing the River Eden not long into its long journey from Dundee to Penzance in October 2011. Arriva are the second holders of the Cross Country franchise, taking it over from Virgin Trains who introduced these units.

In a long-gone scene from January 1973 a Class 101 Metropolitan Cammell DMU departs Ladybank for Dundee. Still standing six years after the end of steam is the water column, and the fine array of semaphore signals would continue to signal trains until 1980.

The North British Railway ceased to be in 1923, but its sign at Ladybank was still warning not to trespass fifty years later. The sign disappeared in the 1980s, but the post still stands.

In this July 1984 photograph, Ladybank station still had its original station seats with cast-iron nameplates. Sadly, these have now all gone. Brush Class 47 No. 47157 passes with an Edinburgh-bound train.

Virgin Cross Country Trains Class 221 Voyager No. 221117 *Sir Henry Morton Stanley* crosses Bow of Fife level crossing on a snowy February morning in 2007, with the Dundee–Penzance service. These Virgin units all carry names of explorers from across the centuries.

A4 Pacific No. 60007 *Sir Nigel Gresley* approaches Bow of Fife level crossing with 'The Coronation' rail tour in May 2009. The train had started in London the day before, behind No. 60163 *Tornado*, with 60007 taking over at York for the run to Edinburgh. This photograph is of the following day's leg from Edinburgh to Dundee. (Graeme Blair)

Springfield station, seen here in May 2014, has been unstaffed for many years, and only four trains per day stop here. The station building is now a private residence.

Fragonset Brush Class 47 No. 47712, formerly named *Lady Diana Spencer*, with classmate No. 47709 on the rear, approaches Springfield station in July 2005, hauling an open golf championship special to Leuchars, from where passengers were bussed to the Old Course at St Andrews. (Graeme Blair)

English Electric Class 55 Deltic No. 55002 *The King's Own Yorkshire Light Infantry* approaches Cupar with 'The Deltic Aberdonian' rail tour from York to Aberdeen and return in April 2014. This loco is owned by the National Railway Museum, and was on its first main-line trip since restoration. (Graeme Blair)

A snowy day in February 1970 sees BRCW Class 26 No. D5306 standing at the home signal at Cupar station. It was piloting a Brush Class 47 on the daily Aberdeen–London service.

Cupar's handsome station, seen here in June 2014, is built to a similar design as Markinch and Ladybank. It houses the Cupar Heritage Centre, which is open three days a week. Cupar signal box, seen in the distance, is the first mechanical signal box that trains coming from Edinburgh pass, the line up to Cupar being controlled from the Edinbugh signalling centre.

A BRCW Class 27 approaches Cupar with a Dundee–Edinburgh service. Many of these services were changed to loco hauled in the 1980s, prior to the new Class 150s arriving. The silo in the background is at the former sugar beet factory, which closed in the 1970s. It was rail connected and had its own steam locomotive.

Leuchars, seen in July 2014, is a busy station serving St Andrews and RAF Leuchars, which is soon to become an Army base. Originally it was a junction, with lines to Tayport and round the Fife coast via St Andrews. Fife coast trains terminated at the, now filled in, bay platform. A siding also went into RAF Leuchars.

Although Leuchars station has been reroofed, the original features remain. This photograph was taken during a quiet spell on a beautiful day in July 2014.

The signal is up for the Aberdeen-bound East Coast HST to depart Leuchars; meanwhile, the other signal is also up for the arrival of a train from Dundee. The signalman in the former junction signal box will have a much quieter shift than in former years.

A1 Pacific No. 60163 *Tornado* heads the Inverness–Edinburgh leg of 'The Cathedrals' express to Scotland rail tour at Leuchars in May 2012. This six-day tour, which started in London, travelled as far north as Kyle of Lochalsh using a number of different steam locomotives. (Graeme Blair)

An East Coast HST approaches St Fort with a London King's Cross–Aberdeen service in August 2014. The bridge abutments on the right once carried the North of Fife line, which joined the main line at St Fort Junction. National Express, like GNER, ran into financial difficulties with this service and handed it back to the DFT.

A First Scot Rail Class 170 No. 170416 passes St Fort station in April 2014. The station closed in 1964 and is now a private residence, while the former yard on the opposite side is now a bus depot.

Direct Rail Services Brush Class 47 No. 47810 *Peter Bath MBE* climbs away from Wormit and the Tay Bridge with a returning Compass Tours 'Forth and Tay Bridges' express bound for Crewe in August 2014. Classmate No. 47501 *Craftsman* is on the rear of the train. (Graeme Blair)

First Scot Rail Class 170 No. 170424 has just crossed the Tay Bridge and is passing Tay Bridge South signal box in May 2014. This box, along with Leuchars and Cupar, is due to remain open until 2025.

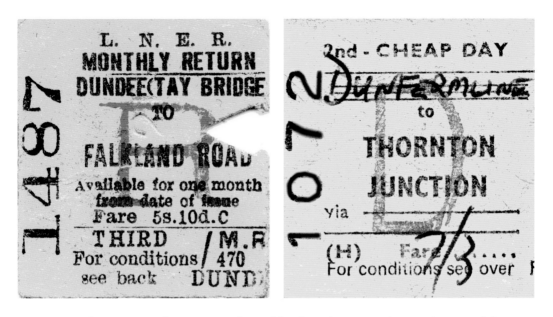

Two return ticket portions. The LNER Dundee–Falkland Road was issued in April 1947 and the Dunfermline–Thornton Junction in December 1968. Both these journeys are no longer possible.

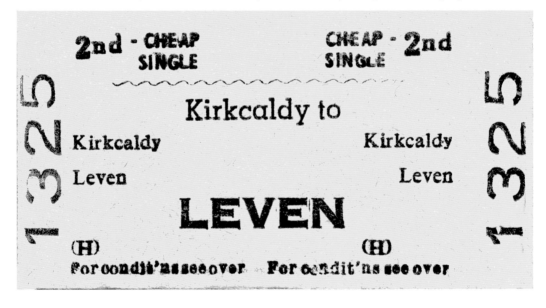

A ticket for a journey that may be possible again if the current campaign to reopen the Leven branch is successful. This ticket was issued in 1968, the year before the branch closed to passengers.

A small number of locomotives have carried names associated with Fife. This is the nameplate of Class 55 Deltic No. D9006 *The Fife and Forfar Yeomanry*. The locomotive was built in 1961 and named at Cupar, the headquarters of the regiment and the then county town, in December 1964. It was withdrawn and scrapped in 1981.

Brush Class 47 No. 47641 *Fife Region* bursts through Forthar Bridge on the climb to Lochmuir Summit with a Cross Country Aberdeen–Plymouth service in November 1990. Built in 1965 it was originally named *Colossus* and was renamed *Saint Columba* in 1996. It was withdrawn and scrapped in 2009.

Glenrothes with Thornton station opened in 1992, belatedly replacing Thornton Junction station, which had closed twenty-three years previously. Here First Scot Rail Class 158 No. 158714 waits to depart Platform 1 for Newcraighall, Edinburgh, via Kirkcaldy. All Fife Circle services use Platform 1 whichever direction they are travelling in, except those that continue on to Markinch, which use Platform 2.

National Express Scot Rail Class 150 No. 150284 approaches Glenrothes with Thornton in May 2002. National Express were the first holders of the Scot Rail franchise at privatisation.

Cardenden, like Lochgelly, the next station along the line, is situated above street level and likewise has no original buildings, only shelters. A First Scot Rail Class 158 arrives with a service from Glenrothes with Thornton to Newcraighall, Edinburgh, in July 2014.

Many of Fife's stations have these barrel train planters, which make a colourful addition to the platforms. This is Lochgelly's, here posing beside a First Scot Rail Class 170 waiting to depart for Newcraighall in July 2014.

Passing high above the town's high street, DBS Class 67 No. 67017 *Arrow* approaches Cowdenbeath station with the evening Edinburgh–Fife commuter train in July 2014. DBS operate this service on behalf of Scot Rail. Interestingly, this locomotive shares the same name and last two digits of its number with a former Britannia Class steam locomotive.

Commuters get off their train at Cowdenbeath and head home in July 2014. The original station buildings have been replaced by more modern ones.

Closed to passengers in 1930, Halbeath station, seen here in July 2014, still stands. It is situated between a level crossing and the eastern end of Townhill Yard, and is abandoned.

Dunfermline's Queen Margaret station stands on the site of Townhill Junction, where the line to Dunfermline Upper and Stirling branched off. It opened in 2000 and is named after the nearby hospital. A First Scot Rail Class 158 No. 158738 arrives with a service to Newcraighall in July 2014.

Dunfermline Town, seen here in July 2014, formerly Dunfermline Lower, is the only station on the branch to retain its original buildings, albeit only on Platform 1. Platform 2 used to be an island platform, but no longer. Where the line used to be is now an access road.

Cast-iron detail under the canopy of Dunfermline Town. Many of Fife's stations now have Gaelic translations on their name boards.

With a characteristic exhaust plume, West Coast Railways Brush Class 47 No. 47854 *Diamond Jubilee* powers through Dunfermline Town with 'The Royal Scotsman' luxury train in August 2014. This is the three-day Highland Tour and it is heading for Boat of Garten on the Speyside Railway, where it will spend the night.

In striking silver livery, DBS Class 67 No. 67026 *Diamond Jubilee* arrives at Rosyth station with the evening commuter train from Edinburgh. Its usual rake of maroon DBS coaches were away for repainting when I took this photograph, in June 2014, and had been replaced by the ex-Virgin Trains coaches seen here.

Photographed on a May evening in 1978, Lochmuir signal box stood at the highest point on the main line through Fife. It controlled a passing loop and crossovers. Slow trains were frequently put in the loop to allow expresses to pass. In steam days, with gradients averaging 1 in 100 from either side, some trains would require banking assistance.

Signalman Jimmy Crichton at work in Lochmuir signal box in the 1960s. Jimmy started his railway career as a surfaceman at Markinch before becoming a signalman in 1947. He worked at Springfield and Falkland Road signal boxes before moving to Lochmuir, a box he served at for nearly twenty years. (David Crichton)

On a May evening in 1978, an English Electric Class 37, on an engineers' train, has been put into the loop at Lochmuir to allow the passage of a Brush Class 47 on an Edinburgh–Aberdeen express. The box and loop closed two years later.

Two BRCW Class 26s accelerate away from Ladybank with an Edinburgh–Inverness train in May 1978. The building to be seen at the end of the train was a wagon repair shop and was only recently demolished after its roof collapsed following heavy snowfall. The signal box closed in 1980 and was soon demolished. (Graeme Blair)

A National Express Scot Rail Class 158 passes the well-known landmark of Collessie church and is about to pass the site of the village's station. The station closed in 1955, when all passenger services on the Ladybank–Perth line were withdrawn.

Lost in the landscape, a First Scot Rail Class 158 skirts Lindores Loch while working a Perth–Edinburgh service. Although no boats were out when this was taken in May 2010, the loch is popular for fishing and also curling during severe winters.

A National Express Scot Rail Class 158 passes the site of Glenburnie Junction in June 2004. This was where the North of Fife line branched off. The Ladybank–Perth line was originally double track, but was singled in 1933, with the exception of the section from Glenburnie Junction to Newburgh which was retained until 1960, when the junction closed.

47

Unusual motive power for 'The Royal Scotsman' in the shape of EWS Class 66 No. 66114 seen here climbing from Newburgh towards Glenburnie in August 2000. Clatchard Quarry in the background used to be rail connected, and supplied many thousands of tons of ballast to the railway.

Brush Class 47 No. 47206 passes Newburgh with an Edinburgh–Inverness service in July 1978. The signal box, loop and yard closed in 1980. (Graeme Blair)

This photograph, taken at Newburgh, shows the first ever working of an HST over the Ladybank–Perth line, in April 1978. A promotional trip prior to the introduction of these trains a few months later, it had already visited Aberdeen and Inverness and was making its way back to Edinburgh. (Graeme Blair)

With Newburgh in the background, BRCW Class 26s Nos 26026 and 26015 have just left Fife and entered Perthshire while working an evening Edinburgh–Inverness service in June 1978. (Graeme Blair)

Opened in 1890, the Forth Bridge was the first major structure to be built from steel. Designed by Henry Fowler and Benjamin Baker, the bridge was financed by the Midland, Great Northern, North Eastern and North British Railway Companies. The main contractor was William Arrol & Co., and 54,000 tons of steel was used in its construction, which took seven years.

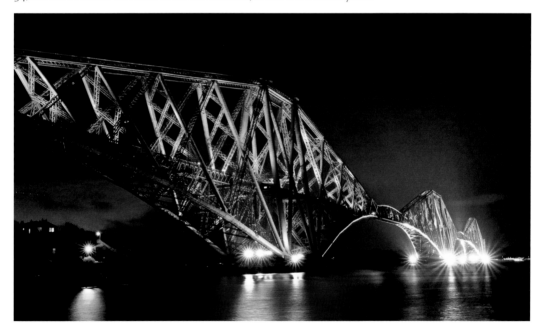

When viewed at night, the Forth Bridge looks even more spectacular. The floodlights were first switched on after a fantastic fireworks display at the culmination of the bridge's centenary celebrations in 1990. The bridge is currently being considered for UNESCO world heritage site status, and Network Rail are planning a visitor centre on the Fife shore.

The Tay Bridge, opened in 1887, replaced the first bridge, which had collapsed during a storm in 1879. Designed by William Barlow and built by William Arrol & Co., construction started in 1883. The original bridge's piers stand as a reminder of the disaster that occurred here.

In this photograph, taken from the west side of the Tay Bridge, the brickwork arches at the Fife end are a fine sight in the sunshine. Like the original bridge, it has a central high girders section to allow the passage of ships. Some parts of the first bridge were used in the construction of the replacement bridge.

Freight traffic has drastically reduced since this shot of a Brush Class 47 heading the daily southbound Freightliner was taken in April 1967. It is about to pass Falkland Road station. The fence in the foreground was a recent addition, replacing the platforms that had been removed the previous year.

A BRCW Class 26 heading the evening southbound parcels train up Falkland Road Bank meets a classmate heading north with a cement train in May 1967.

English Electric Class 40 D253 departs Newburgh with a Perth-bound freight in April 1967. Newburgh still had North British lower quadrant signals at this time. (Graeme Blair)

A British Railways Class 24 passes through Newburgh with a Millerhill–Perth fitted freight, including four new Land Rovers on the leading wagon, in April 1975.

One of Edinbugh Haymarket's English Electric Class 40s works hard on the northbound climb to Lochmuir Summit with a heavy cement train on a May evening in 1970.

A BRCW Class 26 moves forward out of Ladybank yard to join the main line with a ballast train in October 1970. The only things remaining from this scene, apart from the running lines, are the buildings to the right; everything has else has gone, and the signal box and engine shed site is now overgrown with trees.

Still in original livery in September 1970, a BRCW Class 26 approaches Falkland Road station with a northbound mixed fitted freight. The cutting sides were still in a tidy condition at this time.

Moving on to June 2003 and the vegetation is taking over as Rail Freight Class 60 No. 60069 Humphry Davy heads the Linkswood Tanks aviation fuel train, a service that ran weekly until recently, due to the closure of RAF Leuchars.

On a June evening in 1978, English Electric Class 40 No. 40150, heading a northbound cement train, has been put into the Down loop at Ladybank to allow the passage of classmate No. 40007, heading an Edinburgh–Aberdeen express. (Graeme Blair)

Thirty-six years later DBS Class 66 No. 66044 stands in the loop with a diverted china clay empties working to Aberdeen, due to engineering work at Larbert. First Scot Rail Class 170 No. 170451 passes with an Edinburgh–Aberdeen service.

English Electric Class 40 No. 261 enters North Queensferry station, having just crossed the Forth Bridge with an Oxwelmains–Inverness Pressflow cement train in May 1973.

With the dockyard diesel shunter standing by, EWS Class 66 No. 66149 stands in Rosyth Docks coupled to a KUA double-bogie wagon, loaded with a nuclear flask bound for Sellafield, in November 2005. The dockyard crane in the background, a local landmark has since been removed and replaced by a much larger one. (Jules Hathaway)

Thornton diesel depot opened in 1984, fifteen years after Thornton steam shed closed, and is situated at the east end of Thornton marshalling yard. A BRCW Class 26 stands beside the shed in October 1991, showing the shape of things to come, with A4 Pacific No. 60009 *Union of South Africa* in the background. The shed is now 60009's home.

Class 56 No. 56056 passes along the now closed Westfield branch at Kinglassie with an empty MGR working from Longannet to Westfield opencast mine in May 1997. The branch used to extend via Lochore to Kelty, where it joined the Edinburgh–Perth line. (Jules Hathaway)

In February 2003 a trial run from Grangemouth to Cameron Bridge Distillery on the Leven branch was run by DRS for hauliers W. H. Malcolm and Diagio, owners of the distillery. The single wagon was top and tailed by Class 20 No. 20301 and Class 37 No. 37610. Here 20301 stands at the former Cameron Bridge station. (Jules Hathaway)

The trial run down the Leven branch completed, Class 37 No. 37610, with Class 20 No. 20301 on the rear, departs from Thornton Junction on their return run trip to Grangemouth. Nothing ever became of this trial run. (Jules Hathaway)

Pipe trains have been an occasional site in Fife since the seventies, tending to run for a few weeks or months as required. Here, in May 1976 at the beginning of the oil boom, two British Railways Class 25s coast down Falkland Road Bank with one such train.

Another occasional train is the mud oil tanks, a fluid used in the oil drilling industry. This is the empties working, returning from Aberdeen; the loaded train heads north via Stirling and Dundee. It is seen here at Forthar Bridge on the climb to Lochmuir in May 2010, headed by GB Rail Freight Class 66 No. 66701 *Whitemoor*.

Freightliner Heavy Haul Class 66 No. 66601 *The Hope Valley* approaches Cupar station with the Aberdeen–Oxwellmains cement train empties in July 2014. Like the mud oil train, it runs north via Stirling and Dundee. This is the only regular freight train service on the main line through Fife.

In June 1988 a cement train was heading north through Cupar station when part of it became derailed, severely damaging the track and the bridge carrying the B940 across the railway. In this view the damage to the wagons can clearly be seen. The bridge had to be demolished and the temporary footbridge can be seen here. (David Murray)

EWS Class 66 No. 66054 heads a loaded MGR coal train through Inverkeithing station in April 2000. Originating in the west of Scotland, it will travel to Townhill yard, Dunfermline, where the loco will run round before continuing on to Longannet power station via Culross. This practice ceased when the Stirling–Alloa line opened in 2008.

EWS Class 66 No. 66123 skirts the Firth of Forth at Culross in May 2000, and passes Blair Castle with empty cement wagons for Longannet, where they will be loaded with fly ash. They will then travel to a cement works at Westbury in Wiltshire. (Jules Hathaway)

DBS Class 66 No. 66090 passes through Cardenden station in October 2014 en route to Earlseat opencast mine on the Leven branch, where its train will be loaded with coal to be taken to Hunterstone. At the time of writing this is the only train to use the Leven branch and the Dunfermline–Kincardine line. (Graeme Blair)

With the opening of the Stirling–Alloa line, coal trains from the west of Scotland to Longannet had a much shorter distance to travel, and by not having to cross the Forth Bridge they can be longer and heavier. Here, in September 2014, DBS Class 66 No. 66193 approaches Kincardine with imported coal from Hunterston deep water terminal.

The largest industrial railway system in Fife was the Wemyss Private Railway, which served mines in the Methil, Buckhaven and East Wemyss areas. The Michael Colliery disaster in 1967 meant the railway lost most of its traffic, and when the Lochead Colliery closed in 1970 the railway did too. WPR No. 17 departs Methil yard in June 1970.

Andrew Barclay 0-4-0ST No. 3 shunts wagons at the Frances Colliery, Dysart, in February 1971. This was the most common type of locomotive found in the Fife coalfield. They were produced for many years, this one in 1902. The mine closed in 1988, having never resumed production after the 1984 miners' strike.

The 1921-built Pecket 0-4-0ST BAC No. 2 shunts at the British Aluminium works, Burntisland, in 1967, one of two such locomotives at the works. Withdrawn in 1971, the locomotive is preserved at the Yeovil Railway Centre in Somerset. BAC No. 1 is preserved at the Caledonian Railway, Brechin. (David Crichton)

In Lochore Meadows Country Park, in July 2014, standing beside the winding frame of the Mary Pit, which closed in 1966, is former Francis Colliery Andrew Barclay 0-4-0ST No. 30, dating from 1949. Both are reminders of a once great industry.

Falkland Road station is where my interest in railways began, and I still return if there is something special to see. They don't come any more special than this, the Royal Train, headed by Class 67 No. 67006 *Royal Sovereign* carrying Prince Charles and the Duchess of Cornwall south from Aberdeen in June 2009.

Royal Class 67 No. 67005 *Queen's Messenger* brings up the rear of the Royal Train as it climbs to Lochmuir Summit.

In atrocious conditions, preserved English Electric Class 40 No. 40145 heads south with 'The Whistling Scotsman' rail tour in August 2005. This three-day tour, which started in Birmingham, travelled as far north as Inverness and Kyle of Lochalsh. This was the first time in many years that a Class 40 had passed Falkland Road.

A class of diesel that had never passed through Falkland Road before was a Class 52 Western, but that changed in June 2010 when the preserved No. D1015 *Western Champion* came through. The Western was on its way south from Inverness with the returning 'Western Chieftain' rail tour that had started in Birmingham three days earlier.

There are many disused railways in Fife worth exploring, and in the following images I shall give a brief look at nine of them. The Charlestown branch is still intact apart from its connection at Elbowend Junction and the last half mile to Charlestown harbour and station. This milepost marks 1 mile from Elbowend Junction.

The Charlestown branch reopened in 1894 following its rebuilding from a wagonway, but its route was altered to avoid a steep gradient. Walking the branch today is difficult due to overgrown vegetation, but it is accessible at a number of crossings and bridges.

The naval stores at Crombie were served by a short branch, which left the Charlestown branch at Braeside Junction. Trains would travel beyond the junction then reverse in. This bridge carried the Crombie branch across the Lyne Burn. It was traffic to Crombie that kept the Charlestown branch open until 1993.

The end of the line. Beyond this point houses have been built on the trackbed, and where it passed Charlestown harbour there is now a road. This section closed in 1964. The station, which was beyond the harbour, closed to passengers in 1926.

The Fife & Kinross Railway, which ran from Ladybank to Mawcarse Junction on the Edinburgh–Perth line, was fully open by 1858. It had three intermediate stations at Auchtermuchty, Strathmiglo and Gateside. This view at Ladybank station shows the bay platform where trains left from with the buffers, still in place fifty years after the line closed.

The façade and platform of Auchtermuchty station still survive, built into the office block of Sterling's furniture warehouse. The warehouse originally belonged to Rippin Structures. This company started business in the goods shed, then built the shed seen here, which was extended along the trackbed in stages. The section from here to Ladybank was the first to close, in 1957.

Between Strathmiglo and Gateside the railway crosses the River Eden five times, on a mixture of stone and steel girder bridges, of which only the stone ones survive. During the 1920s and 1930s Sentinel steam railcars were used on the line. Passenger services were withdrawn in 1950.

Strathmiglo and Gateside stations survive as private houses. Gateside, seen here, being rather small, has an extension built where the platform once was. The line closed in 1964. The trackbed from Ladybank to Auchtermuchty has virtually disappeared, but west of Auchtermuchty some parts can still be walked.

Leaving the main line at Markinch Junction was the Auchmuty branch. This split at Auchmuty Junction, seen here, with the Leslie branch climbing away to the left to cross Balbirnie Viaduct. Both lines are now cycleways, although the Leslie branch, now called The Boblingen Way, does deviate away from the line in places.

Preston Hall level crossing on the Auchmuty branch still had the rails in place when this photograph was taken in 2007. They were removed just recently. The branch, which served the Tullis Russell paper mills, closed in the early 1990s.

This plaque mounted at the end of Balbirnie Viaduct commemorates the opening of the Leslie Railway in 1861, and the line opening as a cycle track in 2007. The line closed to passengers in 1932 and to freight in 1967.

Trains arriving in Leslie crossed this fine viaduct above the River Leven; this is the view from the station side. From the station a siding led into Fettykill paper mill. To access this, trains would go into the station, then reverse into the siding, which crossed the Leslie–Glenrothes road at a level crossing.

The Newburgh and North of Fife Railway opened in 1909 and ran from Glenburnie Junction, a mile south of Newburgh, to St Fort on the main line. This is the view looking east from the junction. Glenburnie Junction closed in 1960, along with the section to Lindores station.

The three stations on the line, Lindores, Luthrie and Kilmany, all had identical houses; this is the much extended Lindores station house. Serving small communities, passenger numbers were never high, and these services were withdrawn in 1951. The line did, however, prove useful for trains diverted from the Perth–Dundee line.

Large sections of the line have disappeared 'under the plough', leaving bridge abutments like this one near Dunbog standing alone. This bridge is unusual, being constructed from brick, not concrete, which was used extensively on this line.

Like many bridges on the line, this one is built from concrete, but the arch is finished off with five layers of brick beautifully put together. The North of Fife Railway finally closed in 1964, having been open for only fifty-five years.

The Fife Coast Railway opened in stages between 1854 and 1887. It ran from Thornton Junction to Leuchars Junction via Leven Anstruther, Crail and St Andrews. This is Lower Largo Viaduct, the largest on the line. The line had its own express service, 'The Fife Coast Express', which ran from Glasgow to St Andrews.

Unfortunately it isn't possible to cross Lower Largo Viaduct, but this gives a good idea of the view passengers had from the train, looking across Largo Bay. Heading east from Lower Largo, the Fife Coastal Path uses the former trackbed for a short distance.

Photographed from the Fife Coastal Path, this bridge is between Elie and St Monans. Passenger services were withdrawn from the Leven–St Andrews section in 1965, and this section closed completely in 1966.

The piers of the viaduct across the River Eden at Guardbridge, between St Andrews and Leuchars Junction. This section closed completely in 1969, leaving only the Leven line open, but only for freight, as its passenger services were also withdrawn in 1969. The Leven line is still in place, and a campaign to have passenger services restored is under way.

The Cults Lime Works Railway, which opened in 1856, ran from the main line at Springfield to Cults limeworks and involved a climb of 250 feet. Soon after leaving Springfield it crossed the River Eden on this girder bridge. The line had its own locomotives built by Barclay & Hunslet.

The line passed under the main Cupar–Kirkcaldy road at this bridge. From here the steep climb by way of a long horseshoe curve to the limeworks began. Also from here a line diverged off to Pitlessie Maltings. A runaway train crashed into this bridge in 1932 and the railway closed in 1947.

Between Falkland Road and Kingskettle stations the Forthar Lime Works Tramway ran from a loading bank and siding up to what is now Forthar Farm. It passed under the Cupar–Kirkcaldy road by this tunnel.

The tunnel is in remarkably good condition, considering the traffic that passes over it. It was built by the railway at their expense as a sweetener to the landowner, Lord Balfour, across whose land they were building the main line. The tunnel is blocked at the farm end by a Second World War anti-tank defence.

The Dunfermline–Stirling Railway opened as far as Alloa in 1850 and to Stirling in 1852, with trains leaving from Dunfermline Upper. Soon after leaving Dunfermline, the trains crossed this viaduct, one arch of which has been removed where it crossed over a road. What remains of the trackbed between here and William Street is totally overgrown.

Phoenix Lane level crossing also had a footbridge, which still stands – note the gateposts still in place. The crossing keeper's hut is built into the furthest-away uprights of the bridge. I'm sure this bridge would come in handy on a preserved railway. Passenger services on the line were withdrawn in 1968.

Beyond William Street in Dunfermline the trackbed becomes the West Fife Cycle Way and very good it is too, running for 11 miles to a point just outside Clackmannan. It cannot go any further due to the reopening of the line from Stirling to Alloa and Longannet, in 2008. These cyclists are passing Bogside signal box.

The waiting room at Bogside still lurks in the bushes fifty-six years after the last passenger train stopped here. The line west from Bogside closed in 1979 and the section from Bogside to Oakley in 1982. Following the closure of Comrie Colliery, the final section to Dunfermline closed in 1987.

Wormit Tunnel lay at the east end of Wormit station on the line to Tayport and was on a sharp curve. It was here in 1955 that a locomotive running tender first, hauling an excursion train, overturned while exiting the tunnel at excessive speed, derailing four coaches in the process. Three people were killed and many injured.

The building of the approach roads to the Tay Road Bridge meant the closure of the section of the Tayport branch east of Newport in 1966, and the line closed completely in 1969. Happily, Newport East station survives as a house, and Wormit station was moved to the SRPSs Bo'ness & Kinneal Railway.

On 29 December 2013, identical memorials on both sides of the Firth of Tay were unveiled to commemorate the fifty-nine people known to have died in the Tay Bridge disaster on 29 December 1879. This is the memorial on the Fife shore.

This sign at the south end of the Tay Bridge tells the story of the disaster, when the cast-iron columns, of dubious quality, collapsed during a storm, taking down the high girders of the bridge and the train that was crossing at the time. The locomotive, No. 244, was recovered and repaired. It acquired the nickname 'The Diver'.

The Lochty Private Railway opened in 1967, running on the last 1½ miles of the East Fife Central Railway, which ran from Leven to Lochty and had closed in 1964. A4 Pacific No. 60009 *Union of South Africa* was the sole motive power, pulling one of the observation coaches from the LNER Coronation express.

When 60009 returned to the main line in 1973, ex-Wemyss Private Railway Bagnall 0-6-0ST No. 16 was acquired, but having no train brakes, only its own steam brake, it had to propel the train up the hill from Lochty. A second coach had been added by this time. No. 16 is now at the Caledonian Railway, Brechin.

Lochty's last season was in 1991. In February 1992 the 60009 support crew, some of whom were also involved at Lochty, had a last steaming day using Barclay 0-4-0ST Forth, seen here arriving back at Lochty. In the brake van is 60009 chief engineer at the time, the late Lindsay Spittal. My daughter looks on from the signal box.

When Lochty closed, some of those involved formed the Kingdom of Fife Railway Preservation Society, and they now have a base at Kirkland yard, Leven, for their collection of rolling stock and industrial locomotives. Their collection includes this ex-RAF Leuchars, North British 0-4-0 diesel shunter *River Eden*.

A4 Pacific No. 60009 *Union of South Africa*, or No. 9 as it is generally referred to, climbs past Falkland Road in September 1973. This was its third special since returning to the main line earlier in the year. At this time the locomotive was based at Kirkcaldy goods shed.

By 1974 No. 9 had moved to Markinch goods shed, and this was to be its home for the next twenty years, apart from 1990–1992, when it was based at Thornton. The locomotive is seen here in 1974, standing beside Markinch signal box, waiting to leave for Edinburgh to pick up a special for Arbroath.

On a frosty morning in November 1980 No. 9 sets off across Markinch Viaduct for Edinburgh to take over the 'Forth and Tay' express that was coming up from Coventry. This tour was organised by the Severn Valley Railway. Balbirnie Viaduct on the Leslie branch can be seen in the distance.

Over the years much major work was carried out on No. 9 at Markinch 'works', including a full boiler re-tube in 1980. In this photograph the locomotive has been jacked up and is resting on blocks to allow the bogie to be removed for overhaul. (Ian Leven)

No. 9 and K4 2-6-0 No. 61994 *The Great Marquess*, complete with support coach, pass the site of Lumphinnans Central Junction en route to their new home at the former diesel servicing shed at Thornton, in April 2007. No. 9's owner John Cameron had recently acquired the K4, which was fresh from overhaul at Crewe.

K4 2-6-0 No. 61994 *The Great Marquess* stands outside Thornton shed in March 2008. This small but powerful locomotive was built in 1938, one of a class of six that were designed specifically to work the steeply graded West Highland Railway. These locomotives worked on the West Highland Railway until 1959 when they were transferred to the original Thornton depot.

The Great Marquess powers through Kinghorn station in May 2008, with an SRPS Fife Circle rail tour. The locomotive was withdrawn from BR service in 1961 and purchased by Viscount Lord Garnock who used it on a number of special trains in the 1960s.

On the same rail tour as above, *The Great Marquess* climbs through North Queensferry station. For over thirty years, from the early 1970s, the locomotive was based at the Severn Valley Railway, where it worked on the railway and was also used on main-line specials, including taking part in the West Highland Railway centenary in 1994.

Thornton shed plays host to a number of visiting locomotives that call in for fuel, servicing and turning on the nearby triangle. Here, sister locomotive to No. 9, No. 4464 *Bittern*, rests between duties in May 2012. The locomotive had hauled 'The Cathedrals' express to Scotland from York to Perth a few days earlier.

Class 55 Deltic No. 55022 *Royal Scots Grey* stands beside No. 9 in May 2008. The reason for the Deltic's visit was that it was taking part in the opening ceremony of the Alloa line, along with *The Great Marquess*, the two locomotives top and tailing the special train. Unfortunately the shed is not open to the public.

This West Coast Railways Brush Class 47 No. 47760 has brought the 'Great Britain' rail tour across from Edinburgh to Thornton in April 2013, and the train will now be split, with one half going to Fort William and Mallaig behind *The Great Marquess*, and the other half to Kyle of Lochalsh behind an LMS Class 5 4-6-0.

LMS Royal Scot No. 46115 *Scots Guardsman* pokes its nose out of the shed in September 2013. Earlier in the day the locomotive had worked a special, conveying golfing celebrities from Edinburgh to Gleneagles in connection with the 2014 Ryder Cup. The locomotive is a celebrity itself, having starred in the classic 1930s documentary *Night Mail*.

North British Railway J36 No. 673 *Maude* climbs away from Newburgh with 'The Strathearn' express in October 1983. The train ran from Falkirk to Perth via Stirling and returned through Fife and across the Forth Bridge. Built in 1891, the locomotive served in France during the First World War and is named after General Sir Frank Maude. (Graeme Blair)

LNER D49 4-4-0 No. 246 *Morayshire* approaches Thornton with an SRPS rail tour in July 1981 bound for Dundee. Once a common sight in Fife, the Shires were used on many of the local passenger trains. Above the locomotive can be seen the winding towers of ill-fated Rothes Colliery, closed after only four years due to severe flooding.

LNER V2 2-6-2 4771 *Green Arrow* climbs to Lochmuir on its way from Dundee to the National Railway Museum at York in May 1987. The V2, a type once common in Fife, had been taking part in the Tay Bridge centenary celebrations. (David Murray)

LNER A2 Pacific No. 60532 *Blue Peter* heads the SRPS 'Fife Coast' express rail tour out of North Queensferry tunnel in June 1999. This former Dundee-based locomotive was making a welcome return to Fife. This train travelled over the Fife and Edinburgh Suburban Circles.

There was quite a crowd out at Ladybank to see BR Britannia Pacific No. 70013 *Oliver Cromwell* pass with the 'Great Britain Three' in April 2010. This annual rail tour covers most of Britain and is steam hauled all the way. *Oliver Cromwell* was the last operational Pacific locomotive at the end of BR steam.

On a superb August afternoon in 2011, LMS Black 5 4-6-0 No. 45231 *Sherwood Forester* approaches Lochgelly with the second of the day's SRPS Forth Circle rail tours. Over 800 of these versatile locomotives were built.

LMS Royal Scot 4-6-0 46115 *Scots Guardsman* accelerates away from Ladybank with an SRPS rail tour to Inverness in June 2012. This was a type of locomotive very rarely seen in Fife in steam days.

A type of steam locomotive never seen in Fife before is a Great Western Railway Castle Class. This changed in May 2012 when No. 5043 *Earl of Mount Edgcumbe* visited Scotland on a three-day trip which included a trip round the Forth Circle. The locomotive is seen here approaching the former Lumphinnans Central Junction.

On an April evening in 1971, the second man of English Electric Class 40 D352 exchanges the single line token with the Newburgh signalman. This practice ended the following year when the signal box was refurbished and a tokenless block system was introduced.